Does God Have a Son?

Mike Chuks Nwanegbo

DEDICATION

This book is dedicated to all the warriors of righteousness who have risked their lives over generations to bring the gospel of Jesus Christ to the lost. Also to all those who will accept Jesus after reading this book.

TABLE OF CONTENT

ACKNOWLEDGMENTS

The concept that God has a son has generated great controversy in the world. Many including the Muslim see Jesus as the greatest prophet that ever lived but do not see him as the son of God. Some believe that accepting him as the son of God is tantamount to making him equal to God. In this book, I have taken time to do research, question and try to establish whether God has a son or not. The conclusion is yours to make after looking at both sides of the case. I believe that at the end of your reading, you would on your own conclude on whether Jesus is truly the son of God or not. If you are unable to arrive at a conclusion, at least it would spur you to further research on the controversial issue.

DOES GOD HAVE A SON?

Does God have a son? This question has been asked over centuries. Many would also say that if God had a son, then it would mean that he has a wife. How can God have a wife?

I do believe that in order to answer this question, we have to begin by defining who a son is.

Google defines a son as "a boy or man in relation to either or both of his parents. A male descendant "the son of Adam"

Merriam- Webster defines a son as: 1. a male child offspring. 2. A man or boy closely associated with or thought of as a child of something (as a country, race or religion) e.g. son of liberty.

Dictionary.Com defines it as a male child or person in relation to his parents, a male child or person adopted as a son; a person in legal position of a son.

From the above definition a son could be biological or adopted. The Christians call Jesus the son of God. Could this be true? If Jesus is the biological son of God, it means that we should be looking for a mother. If the mother is a physical being, we would be forced to ask such question as; can God mate with a mere mortal?

These are questions the mortal mind is bound to ask. I do not blame man for asking these questions. For me I believe questions are meant to be answered or if you permit me, I would say that every question has an answer hidden somewhere and it is the duty of man to find them out.

I have set my heart to find out if God has a son. One thing I have decided to do is to set aside that I am a Christian and allow myself to discover the truth.

The Moslems get enraged when you refer to Jesus as the son of God. They believe that God wouldn't descend so low to mate with mortal being. As I got to this point, something went through my mind and I think I better put it down. That thing is that God never does anything on earth that concerns man without getting man involved.

I believe that we could begin by finding out who this God is and what he can do. First I will not want to go into this argument on whether this God exists or not. One thing is that all religions believe that there is a God and that he is eternal, omnipotent, omniscience and omnipresence.

For those who do not believe in God I will want to challenge your mind with a few questions. How come that the universe is so ordered with times and seasons and life circles? How do we explain intelligence of cells? The snow knows when to come and go. The new baby knows how to suck the breast without being taught. The human body responds and adjusts to the environment and even tries to defend and preserve self when endangered.

Some claim that the earth was a product of a bang. The question is: what led to that bang. "A force" they would answer; but where did the force come from and who generated the power that activated the force? One thing I do know is that bangs lead to disorder. The universe is too well ordered to be the product of a bang. The universe is ruled by certain well-ordered laws which if is broken lead to very severe consequences.

Well, let us go back to God. All religions believe that God is omnipotent and that he does as he pleases and nothing is impossible for him. It then implies that God can put his seed in any mortal of his choice to bring forth a son according to his will and purpose. It also means that God can choose anyone, adopt and call such a son.

The future as we have been made to understand, can be foretold as in prophesies. If this is so, it means that we are all known before we were born.

I took the bible to try to understand the assumption that God has a son because it is the book that claimed that God has a son. I found out that the prophets in the scriptures foretold things before they came to pass. They foretold the coming of the son of God. They foretold his birth, ministry, death and resurrection. The prophets were so accurate in their predictions. Prophet Isaiah was extremely accurate in his predictions

'The book of Isaiah tells us that before king Cyrus of Persia was born that God already knew him and the pattern of his life and what he was going to do on earth was revealed to prophet Isaiah. With such precision he prophesied about King Cyrus even before his parents were born.

...who says of Cyrus, 'He is my shepherd and will accomplish all that I please; he will say of Jerusalem, "Let it be rebuilt," and of the temple, "Let its foundations be laid. **Isaiah 44:28**
"This is what the LORD says to his anointed, to Cyrus, whose right hand I take hold of to subdue nations before him and to strip kings of their armor, to open doors before him so that gates will not be shut: **vs 1**
I will go before you and will level the mountains; I will break down gates of bronze and cut through bars of iron. **Vs 2**
I will give you hidden treasures, riches stored in secret places, so that you may know that I am the LORD, the God of Israel, who summons you by name. **vs3**
For the sake of Jacob my servant, of Israel my chosen, I summon you by name and bestow on you a title of honor, though you do not acknowledge me." **Vs 4**

This same prophet Isaiah and other prophets prophesied about the coming of the son of God. They prophesied how God was going to send his son to the world to redeem the world. Isaiah was so specific that he even called him God. What a mystery. Why did he refer to this son of God as God? Except this son of God directly proceeded from the loins of God.

"For unto us a child is born, unto us a son is given: and the government shall be upon his shoulder: and his name shall be called Wonderful, Counselor, The mighty God, The everlasting Father, and The Prince of Peace." **Isaiah 9:6.**

The prophet here made it clear that a time will come when a son shall be born to the nation of Israel and he shall be called "the mighty God, the everlasting father, and the Prince of Peace." These are all the names that Jesus was called.

King and prophet, David, did prophecy about the death of this son of God. Hold it here. This is getting too far. How can the son of God die if he is God? God can't die. What is the mystery here?

King David in psalm 2:7 said that

"The lord had said unto me, Thou art my son; this day have I begotten thee"

Solomon the wisest man that ever lived also talked about this son of God. In ***proverbs 30 verse 4*** he wrote

"Who hath ascended up into heaven or descended? Who hath gathered the wind in his fist? Who hath bound the waters in a garment? Who hath established all the ends of the earth? What is his name and what is his son's name, if thou canst tell?"

The above saying of King Solomon is a mystery. It means that King Solomon by his divine wisdom knew that God has a son.

The Bible and the Torah claimed that God has a son and that the son has a name.

In ***Isaiah 9 verse 6,*** the prophet Isaiah declared his names

"…for unto us a child is born, unto us a son is given and the government shall be upon his shoulder; and his name shall be called wonderful, counselor, the mighty God, the everlasting father, the prince of peace"

This is an amazing prophecy from the most reliable Jewish prophet whose prophecies came to pass with accurate precision. The prophet Isaiah confirmed that God has a son and that the government of heaven and earth shall be upon his shoulders. This son was given the name of God which meant that he was to come in the name and authority of God who is meant to be his father. Who is this son of God? Did he come to this earth or is he yet to come?

In the book of Daniel, the great Babylonian King Nebuchadnezzar claimed to have seen a vision of this son of God when he sentenced 3 Jewish boys to death by burning in fire for defying his command to worship his idol.

"Lord I see four men loose, walking in the midst of the fire, and they have no hurt; and the form of the forth is like the son of God. ***Daniel 3:25***

Wait a minute!! How did the king know that God has a son? Had he encountered him before in a vision? He did not say the fourth like another person but he was specific by saying that the fourth was like the son of God.

Further search took me to **Psalm 2 verse 11-12** where King David affirmed that God has a son and anyone who does not accept his son is doomed *"Serve the Lord with fear, rejoice with trembling.*

Kiss the son, lest he be angry and ye perish from the way, when His wrath is kindled but a little." **Psalm 2:11-12.**

John the Baptist, a well known Jewish prophet and also recognized by the Muslims also made a categorical statement stating that God has a son. In the gospel of **John 3:35-36,** John stated:

35 "The Father loveth the son, and hath given all things into his hand."
36 "He that believeth on the son hath everlasting life: and he that believeth not the son shall not see life; but the wrath of God abideth on him"

The above two verses were referring to Jesus Christ. If you read the Gospel of **John chapter 3 from verse 22 to 36** you would understand that John was testifying that Jesus Christ is the son of God sent to bring the word of God to the world. What is worth noting here is that Prophet John the Baptist warned that:

36 "He that believeth on the son hath everlasting life: and he that believeth not the son shall not see life; but the wrath of God abideth on him"
It simply means that refusing to believe in the son of God attracts the wrath of God and such shall not see eternal life.

The bible in the book of **Hebrews 1:1** tells us that God spoke to our fathers through the prophets but in these last days has spoken to us through his son *"God, who at sundry times and in diverse manner spake in time past unto the fathers by the prophets*
2. Hath in these last days spoken unto us by his son, whom he hath appointed heir of all things, by whom also he made the world.

All the above facts tell us that God through the prophets told us that He has a son. Prophet Isaiah confirms to us that the government is going to be upon the shoulder of the son. We also learn that the world was made through the son *(John 1:3)*. This then means that this Son of God had existed before the creation of the world.

Only Jesus claimed that "before Abraham I am" *(John 8:54)* The Jews understood what he meant by saying that. If the son of God existed before the creation of the world, it means that he existed in the spirit. If he created the world and created the first man and woman without the help of man, it means God has the capability to do whatever he desires.

2

WHO IS THIS SON OF GOD?

The Christians call him Jesus the son of God. The Muslims call him prophet Isa. The Muslims refuse to accept that he is the son of God because they could not comprehend how God could have a son. They assume that sons only can come by conjugal relationship. They also argued that God would not mate with human. One thing they do not consider is that God is omnipotent and does as he pleases. God has the capability to create something out of nothing. God did not need to mate with Mary but could simply put the child in her womb.

Let us see what we can find from the birth of Jesus Christ to prove or disprove the claim that he is the son of God. Let s follow a conversation between Mary and angel Gabriel about the birth of Christ. Angel Gabriel was sent to Nazareth to a virgin called marry and the following conversation ensued.

"and the angel said unto her, fear not Mary; for thou has found favor with God

31. and behold, thou shalt conceive in thy womb, and bring forth a son, and shall call his name Jesus.

32. He shall be great, and shall be called the son of the highest and the Lord shall give him the throne of his father David" **Luke 1vs 30.**

In the above verse, the Messenger of God, Angel Gabriel called said that he shall be called the son of the Highest. The angel only spoke what God told him to say and if that is the case, it means that God himself first introduced Jesus as his son.

Let us continue reading the above Chapter from **verse 33**

33. *"And he shall reign over the house of Jacob forever and his kingdom,*

there shall be no end.
34. *Then said Mary unto the angel, how shall this be seeing that I know not
a man?*

Is Mary's question here familiar with our thought? The normal question we
would all ask is, how can a virgin conceive without a man? The next verse
clearly answers all the questions and clears the confusions.
35. *"And the angel answered and said unto her, the Holy Spirit shall over-
shadow thee: therefore also that Holy thing which shall be born of thee shall
be called the Son of God."*

In **verse 35** above, the mystery of the deity of Jesus was revealed. The
Spirit of God is God. The power of God can do anything. Both the spirit
and power ushered in Jesus by the power of God into the womb of Mary.
Twice in this short passage the angel Gabriel confirmed that Jesus is the
son of God. If we refuse to believe the testimony of man, at least we
should believe the testimony of the angel whom we know as the messenger
of God.

The Angel ended with a conclusive statement to nail the doubt of Mary on
how the message could be possible.
Verse 37 says *"with God nothing shall be impossible"*

The birth of Jesus Christ was a fulfillment of an age long prophecy that
God was going to send his Son, born of a virgin, to save the world. This
long expected messiah is Jesus Christ to be known and addressed as the
Son of God because he came from God and by the mysteries of God
was he born. No human could ever claim to be the father of Jesus. God
through his omnipotent power planted Jesus into the womb of Mary and
to be born at the fullness of time.

God's Testimonies About Jesus Christ
God, long time ago, spoke through the prophets that his word was going

to become flesh and dwell among men. He proclaimed that his son would be born of a virgin. He was so specific that he told us where his son was going to be born, where he would spend his early years and where he was going to do his ministry and how he was going to die and resurrect after three days. God was so specific that he described Jesus' death so vividly thousands of years before he was born.

During Jesus ministry on earth, God spoke clearly and declared Jesus to be his Son. Not only his son but his beloved son.
Matthew 3 vs 16-17:
16 "and Jesus when he was baptized went up straight out of the waters and lo the heavens were opened unto him and he saw the spirit of God descending like a dove and lighting upon him
17. And lo a voice from heaven saying, this is my beloved son in whom I am well pleased"

The above two verses confirmed that God spoke with an audible voice to proclaim to men that Jesus is his son. Why was God interested in doing this? It is clear that God had to point to us that he has a son and that son is his only beloved with whom he is well pleased. By this, God is also saying that his son is the only way to pleasing him.

In *Matthew Chapter 17 verse 1-6,* the bible told the story of the transfiguration. At the mount of transfiguration, God, for a second time, confirmed that Jesus is his beloved son with whom he is well pleased. He ended by urging the people to listen to Jesus.
"while he yet spake, behold, a bright cloud overshadowed them: and behold a voice out of the cloud, which said, This is my beloved son, in whom I am well pleased, hear ye him.
And when the disciples heard it, they fell on their face, and were sore afraid."
Matthew 17 verse 5-6.

Jesus Testimony about himself as the son of God.
Several people have argued that Jesus never called himself the son of

God. The bible has several evidence of Jesus calling himself the son of God. The Jews understood the implication of Jesus calling himself the son of God. According to the prophets, the one who is to come as the son of God will be the messiah and will be God.

In ***Mark 14:61,*** the high priest while questioning Jesus, the night he was arrested, asked

"Art thou the Christ, the son of the blessed?"

Jesus answered *"I am."*

Jesus confirming his true identity to the high priest was absolute declaration of his true identity. The high priest was the absolute spiritual authority in the land. His proclamation is usually final. He refused Christ's confession of self by tearing his garment. That did not change the fact that Jesus had proclaimed to the highest spiritual authority in Israel that he is the long expected messiah; the son of God. The high priest called Jesus' Testimony of self as the son of God, a blasphemy. The same applies today. So many still refer to Jesus testimony of self as a blasphemy.

In ***Math 16:15 –17,*** Jesus posed a question to his disciples after they had given Jesus the opinion of who the people think he is.

"But whom say je that I am?" **Verse 15.**

Apostle Peter in his usual manner was the first to answer.

"Thou art the Christ the son of the living God," **Verse 16.** In response Jesus said to Peter.

"Blessed art thou Simon Barjons for flesh and blood hath not revealed it unto thee but my father which is in heaven." **Verse 17**

By this Jesus was saying that he is the son of God and God in heaven is his father. Another implication of this statement is that whosoever recognizes Jesus as the son of God and the messiah will be blessed. It also implies that the revelation of the true identity of Jesus can only come by revelation from God the father.

Mathew 27: 43 tells us that while Jesus was hanging on the cross the people challenged him to free himself if he was the son of God that he claimed to be.

"He trusted in God: let him deliver him now for he said I am the son of God." By this statement the people were confirming that Jesus called himself the son of God.

In ***John 4: 25 – 26,*** Jesus revealed his true identity to a woman by the well. He was upfront to declare that he is the messiah. As you know we had earlier learnt from the high priest that the messiah was to be called the son of God.

"The woman said unto him, I know that messiah cometh which is called Christ. When he is come, he will tell us all things." **Verse 25** *"Jesus said unto her, I that speak unto thee am he."* **Verse 26**

The gospel of ***John chapter 9: 35:41*** told the story of a man that was born blind. That he was healed by Jesus and the rulers of Israel refused to accept the miracle and cast the man out of the synagogue. Jesus met him and said unto him.

"Do thou believe in the son of God?" **Verse 35** - The young man answered and said: **Verse 36** - *"Who is he Lord that I might believe in him."*

In **verse 37**, *Jesus said unto the young man*

"Thou hast both seen him and it is he that talketh with thee". By the above statement Jesus was confirming that he is the son of God.

3

JESUS CALLED GOD HIS FATHER

I n *John 10 :32,* Jesus claimed that all his works were from God His father. "Many good works have I showed you from my father." This angered the Jews because they did understand that whoever will come as the Christ will be the son of God and thus God. – *"The Jews answered him saying for a good work we stone thee not but for blasphemy and because that thou being a man makest thyself God." – verse 35*

 In the above passage, Jesus did not directly called himself God but that God is his father. But the Jews understood the implication of his statement according to the writing of the prophets.

The same scenario occurred in *John 5:17-23*

"But Jesus answered them, my father worketh hitherto, and I work."

18 "Therefore the Jews sought the more to kill him because he not only had broken the Sabbath, but said also that God was his father, making himself equal with God."

19 "Then answered Jesus and said unto them, verily, verily, I say unto you, the son can do nothing of himself but what he seeth the father do."

20 "For the father loveth the son and showth him all things that himself doeth". Jesus went further to explain his relationship with his father in heaven.

21 "For as the father raiseth up the dead, and quickeneth them, even so the son quickeneth whom he will."

22 "For the father Judgeth no man but hath committed all judgment unto the son."

23 "That all men should honor the son, even as they honor the father. He that honoureth not the son, honoureth not the father which sent him."

These verses are self-explanatory. Judgment is in the hand of the son. If you still do not believe that Jesus is the son of God, what are you going to do on the Day of Judgment because you must face him whom you have denied?

How can you claim to honor God when you refuse to honor one he called his only begotten son.

By this knowledge you are to be blamed if you continue to refuse that Jesus is the son of God. The simple believe in the fact that Jesus is the son of God and the savior of mankind transfers you from eternal death to eternal life. Jesus confirmed this with his own mouth.

"Verily, verily, I say unto you, He that heareth my word and believeth on him that sent me, hath everlasting life and shall not come into condemnation; but is passed from death unto life." – *John 5:24*

In *John 5 verse 26-27*, Jesus went further to say

26 "For as the father hath life in himself so hath he given to the son to have life in himself

27 And hath given him authority to execute judgment also because he is the son of man".

For those who simply believe that Jesus is just a prophet, one unique thing is clear to all; the prophets spoke from what they heard God say. If you do not believe that Jesus is the son of God wouldn't it be simple logic to believe what he said about himself that he is the son of God, if you consider him just as a prophet and you believe the prophets, it implies that God called him his son because the prophets said so.

Some would argue that if Jesus was or is the son of God, how come he died on the cross. To such people, God can't die. Well of a truth, God can't die but it was appointed unto Jesus to lay down his life for 3 days as a sacrifice for the redemption of mankind. Even the prophets foretold this before it came to pass. Jesus did not remain dead, he rose from death after 3 days in order to obey God the father and fulfill prophecy. This same Jesus is alive today. He has shown himself to many people even in this present age. Many Muslims have testified seeing Jesus appearing to them and leading them to the bible, which is the book of eternal life.

I pray that as you read this book that the spirit of Christ will touch your heart to believe in Christ so that you will enjoy eternal life.

Many believe that God is love. If this is true which I believe is, then we could explain why Jesus spent most of his years teaching about love and the kingdom of God. He is the only one that taught us to love our neighbor as we love ourselves and also to love our enemies and forgive them that offend us. Almost all religions believe that Jesus was the most perfect of all that came before him. If he was the most perfect and he told us that he is the son of God, why do we doubt him? Jesus never told a lie in his life time; how come we believe almost all he said but do not believe he is the son of God?

In *John 16:15* Jesus claimed that *"All things the father hath are mine"*. By this Jesus was claiming the full right as the only begotten son of God. What he was saying is that he is the true and undisputable son of God. You can read also *John 3:16-18, 34-36, John 5:19,20,25,26, John 6:40,* and *John 11:4.*

OTHER PEOPLE'S TESTIMONY ABOUT JESUS

In this write up I am going to look at the testimony of those that existed at the time of Jesus especially those that saw him and listened to him. Peter was one of the followers of Jesus Christ.

In the book of **Matthew 16:13 – 17,** Jesus asked an amazing question to his disciples who had been with him for a while. The question was to find out other people's view about him. Many felt he was just a prophet. *"Some say thou art John the Baptist; some, Elijah and others, Jeremiah, or one of the prophets."(**Matthew 16: 14**).* This same view has not changed till date. Several people still see Jesus as a prophet. The truth is that Jesus is more than a prophet.

In response to Jesus' question of

*"Who do men say I the son of man am?"(**Matthew 16: 13b**)*

Peter answered *"Thou art the Christ, the son of the living God." (**Matthew 16:16**)*

How did Peter come to this knowledge? Well we can say that Peter had been with Jesus and had seen all the miracles he had performed. One could argue that many also saw all the miracles but did not see him as the son of God. Jesus revealed the mystery of Peter's confession in **Verse 17** when he said *"flesh and blood hath not revealed it unto thee, but my father which is in heaven." (**Matthew 16:17**).*

By the above statement Jesus was saying that no human can properly explain to any man and convince such that Jesus is the son of the living

God. Such truth can only come from God allowing the Holy Spirit to reveal this truth to an individual or group of people. Only God can give you the grace to accept this truth because it does not make human sense. If you want to know whether Jesus is the son of God, the best is to pray and ask God to make it clear to you. Flesh and blood cannot give you the revelation of Christ as the son of God.

My prayer for you as you read through this write-up is that God will open your spiritual understanding to see Jesus as the son of God or as God the son.

The second Testimony is the testimony of a well-known prophet during the time of Jesus Christ. The name of the prophet is John the Baptist. The whole Jewish nation knew and acknowledged him as a prophet. One thing we know is that true prophets speak the mind of God.

Hebrews 1 :1-2 Says that *"God, who at sundry times and in diverse manners spoke in time past unto the fathers by the prophet."*

"Hath in these last days spoken unto us by his son, whom he hath appointed heir of all things by whom also he made the worlds".

John the Baptist spoke about Jesus. What did he say about Jesus?

In the gospel of *John 1:33 – 34,* John the Baptist bore witness of who Jesus is.

33"And I knew him not: but he that sent me to baptize with water, the same said unto me, upon whom thou shalt see the spirit descending, and remaining on him, the same is he which baptizeth with the Holy Spirit."

34"And I saw, and bare record that this is the son of God".

This true prophet of God who was sent to prepare the way for Christ saw him and recognized him by the spirit and had the boldness to truly call him the son of God. By implication of who a true prophet is, it means that God called Jesus his son through the mouth of the prophet. This testimony of John the Baptist is true and indisputable.

Many that followed him to the end did so because they were sure that he is the son of God.

In *John 1: 49* Nathanael, being led by the spirit of God, on seeing Jesus

and hearing him declared :
"Thou art the son of God: thou art the king of Israel."

How did Nathaniel come to such a quick conclusion? He was led by the spirit of God. Martha, one of the followers of Jesus openly confessed that Jesus is the son of God. In **Matthew 11:27** she said:
"I believe that thou art the Christ, the son of God, which should come into the world."

The implication of the above statement is that the Jews knew that God has a son and that son is going to come as the messiah of Israel and the whole world. The Jews missed it when Jesus came into the earth in humility. He was born into poverty and not into royalty. He mixed with sinners and not the religious leaders. The leaders were looking for the messiah in royalty but he came in humility so they rejected him.
 Another interesting testimony is that of the centurion that supervised his crucifixion. Now listen to his testimony from a roman soldier.
Matthew 27:54 *"Now when the centurion and they that were with him watching Jesus, saw the earthquake, and those things that were done, they feared greatly, saying, truly this is the son of God. "*

What did this hardened Roman soldier see that made him call Jesus the son of God? A Roman soldier calling Jesus the son of God! He saw the earthquake announcing the activity of the day. He saw Jesus praying and forgiving his murderers even in his pain. He saw love that was beyond human. He heard Jesus promising the thief that heaven was sure for him. He heard Jesus calling God his father. The experience was so overwhelming that the centurion confessed against his earlier belief by saying that
"...truly this is the son of God"

David told us that God has a son. Solomon told us that God has a son. Prophet Isaiah clearly told us that God has a son and that the son will be born into the world to redeem mankind. Isaiah went further to tell us how that son of God is going to die. Finally, Prophet John the Baptist not only talked about him but identified him when he saw him.

The conclusion of the matter is that God has a son. He came as flesh, died as a sacrifice on the cross at Calvary, on the third day he rose from death and ascended to heaven where he is seated at the right hand of God the father. He is coming again to judge the living and the dead. Whether you like it or not, you are going to meet him someday and face his judgment.

Today if you will accept this Jesus as the son of God and claim his death for you as a sacrifice for your sins, you will be saved. Jesus is alive and is ready to cleanse you from your sins and help you live by his spirit and will give you eternal life. Yes God has a son and his name is Jesus Christ the messiah.

5

WHAT REJECTING JESUS MEANS

In the gospel of *John 3 verse 18*, Jesus personally said that:
"He that believeth in him is not condemned: but he that believeth not is condemned already, because he hath not believed in the name of the only begotten son of God".
This is a mystery that we must accept by faith. Many that have had death experience and had returned to life have testified this fact that without Jesus, there is no eternal life.
John 3 verse 36 further emphasized this truth by saying
"He that believeth on the son hath everlasting life: and he that believeth not the son shall not see life; but the wrath of God abideth on him"

Could it be that in all your goodness and sacrifices in life, that still the wrath of God is on you and you have not pleased him because you have rejected his son whom he has provided for the salvation of Mankind.
In *John 8:24,* Jesus made another scary statement:
"I said therefore unto you, that ye shall die in your sins: for if ye believe not that I am he, ye shall die in your sin"

This is serious. The implication of this is that nothing can wipe away your sin except the blood of Jesus. No atonement, suffering, penance and good works can wipe away your sins; only the blood of Jesus. The question is why do people find it difficult to accept? Jesus is the only one who was openly forgiving sins and he is still doing it today. Why not accept forgiveness without labor. Jesus is the only one that can genuinely forgive you and it becomes so in eternity.

John the apostle in his epistle said:
"Who is a liar but he that denieth that Jesus is the Christ? He is antichrist that denieth the father and the son.
Whosoever denieth the son, the same hath not the father; (but) he that acknowledgeth the son hath the father also" **(1 John 2: 22-23.)**
This means that whosoever claims to serve God and denies Jesus does not serve God the father; but is a liar.
I rest my case.

If you accept Jesus as the son of God today, then accept him into your life and permit him to forgive you your sins and give you eternal life. Only through Jesus can you receive forgiveness of sin and eternal life.
After my research, I have come to the full conclusion that God has a son and his name is Jesus Christ. He walked this earth in Israel and was crucified during the time of Pontius Pilate. He resurrected from death on the third day and ascended into heaven. He promised to come back to redeem those who believe in him and judge the living and the dead. It is left to you to decide today. If you want to accept Jesus now, you can tell him now that you accept him. He hears all things. He will hear you and accept you.

If you don't know what to say, maybe this will guide you:
'God I am a sinner. I accept that Jesus is your son, that he came in the flesh, died on the cross, was buried but rose on the third day, ascended to heaven and will come again. I believe that through Jesus my sins will be forgiven. Forgive me for rejecting Jesus and wash away my sin. This day I accept Jesus into my life as my Lord and personal savior. Write my name in your book of life in Jesus name Amen.'
Now that you have received Jesus, God has accepted you and given you the right to be called a son of God. Welcome to the family of God.

About the Author

Mike Chuks Nwanegbo is a pastor in the Redeemed Christian Church of God. He is presently the Coordinator of RCCG Belgium Mission. He is a graduate of University of Port-Harcourt and an ex-student of the Continental Theology Seminal Brussels. He is a Pastor, teacher of the Word, motivational speaker, and recording artist. Mike Chuks Nwanegbo believes in moving people to Godly excellence with focus on making heaven at all cost. He is married to Pastor (Mrs) Boma Nwanegbo and they are blessed with three lovely children; Gloria, Praise and Redeemed.

9 798633 593631